Creation Sings A Lullaby

Nicole Forsythe

WestBow Press books may be ordered through booksellers or by contacting:

WestBow Press
A Division of Thomas Nelson & Zondervan
1663 Liberty Drive
Bloomington, IN 47403
www.westbowpress.com
844-714-3454

ISBN: 978-1-6642-6761-9 (sc)
ISBN: 978-1-6642-6763-3 (hc)
ISBN: 978-1-6642-6762-6 (e)

Library of Congress Control Number: 2022909889

Print information available on the last page.

WestBow Press rev. date: 11/02/2022

WESTBOW
PRESS®
A DIVISION OF THOMAS NELSON
& ZONDERVAN

Dedication

I dedicate this book to all God's precious children and especially to my precious grandson Dominick and all my future grandchildren.

Every morning with the rising sun
comes a brand new day that's just begun.

God looks down with a heart full of love
and makes the sun shine from above.

From the highest mountains to the oceans deep
The whole world wakes from a goodnight's sleep.

Butterflies dance in the warm morning breeze
While colorful birds are chirping in the trees.

Bees are busy buzzing along
And everyone's singing a happy song.

Children are playing in the summer sun
Laughing, smiling, having fun!

Soon the sun will fade away
And the sky will turn a pinkish gray.

The moon will come out in the dark of the night
With the shining stars that twinkle bright.

You'll know the day's over when you see the moon,
And the whip-poor-whistles a good night tune.

Together, the whole world praises God above
To thank him for His marvelous love.

Like a beautiful melody echoing up to the sky
All of creation sings a lullaby.

Farm animals lift their voices and sing
Glorious praises to Jesus our King.

Chickens cluck and cows moo,
Frogs ribbit and owls whoo, whoo, whoo!

Cats meow and dogs bark,
Fireflies softly light up the dark.

Ducks quack and turkeys gobble,
Sheep say baa and geese wobble.

Pigs say oink and rabbits hop,
Chipmunks chitter and fish flop.

Raccoons whimper and beavers chew,
Goats like to spit and roosters cock-a-doodle-doo.

Horses say neigh and donkeys hee-haw,
Birds softly tweet and crows loudly caw.

From the jungle treetops to the swampy ground,
Each and every animal makes their own sound.

Elephants trump and bears growl,
Lions roar and wolves howl.

Tigers purr and crocodiles snap,
Zebras snort and bats flap.

Giraffes hum and pandas eat bamboo,
Kangaroos have pouches and
monkeys say ooh, ooh, ooh!

Hippos yawn and parakeets squawk,
Cheetahs run fast and parrots talk.

The ocean joins in with a majestic song
And crashing waves that are big and strong.

Holding many sea creatures— both great and small:
Some swim, some float, while others crawl.

Dolphins jump and splash about,
Whales blow water out of their spout.

Fish swim fast and seals clap,
Lobsters and crabs like to snippety-snap.
Octopuses crawl and eels wiggle,
Sea horses float and jellyfish jiggle.

What a beautiful world God made for you and me,
Filled with wondrous creatures— land and sea!

I kneel down by my bed and pray,
"Thank you, God, for this wonderful day!"

From the highest mountains to the oceans deep,
The whole world settles for a good night's sleep.

I'm warm and cozy, tucked in my bed,
With my fluffy pillow under my head.

As I drift– wandering in my imagination,
I'll dream of God's beautiful creation.

In the morning I'll wake with the rising sun
To a brand new day that's filled with fun.

Goodnight!

Printed in the United States
by Baker & Taylor Publisher Services